AF480675

PATRIOTIC SPIRITS

INSPIRING A NATION THROUGH POSITIVE THINKING

DR. MINAKSHI BANSAL

DEDICATION

This book is dedicated to the spirited individuals who embody the essence of patriotism and positivity, and to the tireless advocates for unity and progress within our communities. May your dedication inspire a brighter future for our nation.

• • •

Contents

Contents

Contents

Prayer

"Om Bhadram Karnebhih Shrinuyama Devah
Bhadram Pashyemakshabhiryajatrah
Sthirairangais Tushtuvamsastanubhih
Vyashema Devahitam Yadayuh
Svasti Na Indro Vriddhashravah
Svasti Nah Pusha Vishwavedah
Svasti Nastarkshyo Arishtanemih
Svasti No Brihaspatir Dadhatu
Om Shantih Shantih Shantih"

This mantra is a prayer for universal well-being, invoking the blessings of various deities for protection, health, and happiness. It emphasizes the importance of experiencing the auspicious through all senses and living a life aligned with divine purpose. The repetition of "Shantih" at the end signifies a deep desire for peace in the individual, the environment, and the universe at large. This mantra is often recited as a prayer for peace, prosperity, and the physical and spiritual well-being of all beings.

• • •

About The Author

Dr. Minakshi Bansal, born in the bustling metropolis of Delhi, India, has led a life steeped in artistry, scholarly pursuit, and an unwavering commitment to societal betterment. Following her marriage, she relocated to Ahmedabad, Gujarat, where she has since blossomed into a multifaceted beacon of inspiration for many. Dr. Minakshi is not only recognized as a gifted artist in the realm of Fine Arts but also as an esteemed author, a devoted social worker and a dedicated research scholar in Psychology. Her journey, marked by a profound dedication to elevating those around her, especially the downtrodden and underprivileged children of society, is a testament to her deep-seated belief in the transformative power of engagement and empathy.

From her earliest days, Minakshi was distinguished by an insatiable appetite for reading. Her literary universe was inhabited by characters and narratives that spanned ethical tales, motivational and inspirational stories, and the mythic parables imbued with life lessons. This voracious reading habit was not merely for personal edification but was driven by a desire to distill and disseminate the essence of these narratives to foster the development of students and peers alike. She was particularly captivated by the lives and teachings of historical figures and spiritual leaders such as Adi Shankaracharya, Swami Vivekananda, Dr. APJ Abdul Kalam, Mahamana Pandit Madan Mohan Malviya, Mahatma Gandhi, Sardar Vallabhai Patel, and Vinoba Bhave, among others. Their philosophies and life stories fueled her ambition to embody their ideals of resilience, selflessness, and relentless pursuit of knowledge.

Dr. Minakshi's academic and practical engagement with psychology has been equally noteworthy. As a research scholar, her focus has been on exploring the intricate tapestry of the human psyche, aiming to unlock the potential for psychological well-being and societal harmony. Her scholarly work is complemented by her active involvement in social work, where she employs her academic insights to make tangible differences in the lives of the underprivileged. Her endeavours in social work are characterized by an innovative approach that combines traditional wisdom with contemporary psychological practices to address the multifaceted challenges faced by these communities.

Her artistic talents, another facet of her diverse capabilities, are not merely a personal passion but also serve as a medium through which she communicates and connects with others. Her art, rich in symbolism and emotional depth, reflects her philosophical inquiries and social concerns, offering viewers a glimpse into the breadth of her intellect and the depth of her compassion.

In addition to her contributions to the arts and social sciences, Dr. Minakshi has embraced the healing arts of Pranic Healing, mastering the techniques developed by Master Choa Kok Sui. This practice, which focuses on the manipulation of Prana or life energy to heal the body and aura, has been both a personal journey of discovery and a means through which she extends her healing touch to others. Her proficiency in Pranic Healing is complemented by her advocacy and teaching of various forms of meditation aimed at rejuvenation, personal betterment, and the cultivation of harmony within individuals and communities alike.

Dr. Minakshi's life is a narrative of relentless pursuit, not just of personal achievement but of the upliftment and empowerment of society at large. Her diverse interests and talents—spanning the arts, literature, psychology, and the healing practices—converge on a singular path of service. She embodies the spirit of the luminaries who inspired her, channelling their legacy through her actions and teachings. Through her books, art, and social initiatives, she continues to inspire a new generation to embark on their own journeys of self-discovery, resilience, and altruism.

Her commitment to social betterment, particularly her focus on uplifting underprivileged children, reflects a deep understanding of the transformative potential of education and personal development. By integrating her knowledge of psychology, her artistic sensibilities, and her healing practices, Dr. Bansal has developed a holistic approach to social work that addresses both the immediate needs and the long-term well-being of the communities she serves.

As an author, Dr. Minakshi's writings offer a blend of inspirational insights, practical wisdom, and reflective contemplations drawn from her extensive reading and life experiences. Her books serve as a guide for those seeking to navigate the complexities of life with grace, resilience, and purpose. Through her narratives, she extends an invitation to her readers to explore the depths of their own potential and to contribute meaningfully to the collective well-being of society.

In Dr. Minakshi Bansal, we find a remarkable synthesis of the artist, the scholar, the healer, and the social activist. Her life's work stands as a beacon of hope and a source of inspiration for individuals seeking to make a difference in the world. Her story is a compelling reminder of the power of individual action, rooted in compassion and driven by a profound commitment to the betterment of humanity. Dr. Minakshi's legacy is not just in the tangible outcomes of her efforts but in the enduring spirit of inquiry, empathy, and service that she embodies.

• • •

CHAPTER I

The Roots of Patriotism: Understanding National Identity

Patriotism, a sentiment that binds individuals to their nation, is deeply rooted in the understanding and appreciation of one's national identity. This identity is formed through shared histories, common values, traditions, and cultural heritage that collectively shape the societal ethos and individual perceptions of belonging and loyalty to a country.

National identity begins with history, where the tales of founding fathers, significant battles, and historical milestones are more than just chapters in textbooks; they are the threads that weave the fabric of a nation's collective memory. These stories, often glorified and sometimes painful, teach us about resilience, sacrifice, and the visionary ideals that have shaped our present. For instance, the struggle for independence, whether it was against colonial powers or oppressive regimes, plays a pivotal role in defining a nation's spirit and instills a sense of pride and ownership among its citizens.

In addition to historical narratives, national identity is also significantly influenced by cultural heritage. This includes languages, dialects, folklore, music, dance, and art, which are not only expressions of creativity but also mediums through which national narratives are preserved and communicated. Cultural festivals and traditions that bring people together, regardless of their diverse backgrounds, play a crucial role in reinforcing this identity and fostering a sense of unity.

The values that emerge from a nation's constitution, legal frameworks, and public discourses further cement its identity.

These values, such as freedom, justice, equality, and fraternity, often reflect the aspirations of a nation and guide its citizens in their daily lives and interactions with each other and the state. They also shape the national character and influence how citizens perceive their roles and responsibilities towards their country and fellow citizens.

Moreover, the natural landscapes and geographical boundaries of a country contribute to its national identity. The mountains, rivers, forests, and coasts are not just physical features; they are sources of national pride and are often imbued with symbolic meanings and memories. They also play a role in shaping the lifestyles and economic activities of the people, further linking their identity to the land they inhabit.

Education plays a crucial role in nurturing patriotism. Schools are arenas where young minds first learn about their nation's past, the sacrifices made by their ancestors, and the values that their society upholds. This education is not merely academic; it is a socialization process that instills a sense of duty and loyalty toward the country. Through curricula that emphasize civic education, children learn the importance of participation in democracy, respect for the law, and the duties of citizenship.

Media, too, has a powerful impact on national identity. Through the portrayal of national stories, documentaries, and news, media shapes perceptions and attitudes towards the nation. Positive media representation can reinforce national pride and unity, while negative representation can lead to disillusionment and disunity. Hence, responsible media practices are essential for the healthy development of national identity.

Community initiatives that encourage dialogue and interaction among diverse groups also enhance national identity. These initiatives can bridge gaps, heal historical wounds, and foster a sense of belonging among all citizens. Community leaders, NGOs, and civic groups play pivotal roles in these processes, facilitating discussions and activities that highlight the shared values and common goals of the nation.

As we delve deeper into the roots of patriotism, it becomes clear that understanding and appreciating one's national identity is not a passive process but an active engagement. It involves learning about the past, participating in cultural and civic activities, and contributing to the nation's future. This understanding fosters a patriotism that is informed, inclusive, and forward-looking—qualities that are essential for the ongoing development and unity of any nation.

• • •

"True patriotism isn't about blind loyalty; it's about understanding our shared history and striving for a future that honors that legacy. It calls us to be custodians of our past and architects of our future. Let us embrace this duty with both pride and responsibility."

• • •

CHAPTER II

Pride in the Past: Lessons from Our History

Historical consciousness forms a crucial part of any nation's identity, serving as a mirror reflecting the achievements, trials, and aspirations of its people. Delving into the history of a nation not only fosters a sense of pride but also imparts valuable lessons that can guide current and future generations. This deep connection with the past ensures that the lessons learned and the pride felt are not just fleeting emotions but enduring influences that shape national character and decision-making.

The stories of past leaders, philosophers, scientists, artists, and revolutionaries illuminate the pathways they carved in pursuit of liberty, knowledge, and justice. These figures, often elevated to heroic status, become sources of inspiration, their lives painted as exemplars of courage, intellect, and virtue. By studying their journeys, citizens not only develop a sense of continuity and connection with their forebears but also derive practical lessons on resilience and ethical leadership.

Historical milestones such as the signing of a peace treaty, the adoption of a constitution, or a moment of monumental scientific achievement are not just dates in a calendar. They are pivotal moments that have defined the nation's trajectory. Celebrating these achievements during national holidays and through public memorials serves as a reminder of the country's capabilities and potential. It instills a collective memory of success and unity that can motivate citizens to replicate such triumphs in their own pursuits.

However, history is not solely composed of triumphs. It also includes periods of strife, injustice, and errors that have led to suffering and division. It is crucial for a nation to acknowledge these darker periods openly and learn from them. This involves examining the circumstances that led to such outcomes, the roles played by different actors, and the impacts on various communities. By confronting and discussing these aspects of history, a nation can foster a more inclusive and empathetic society that is keen to avoid past mistakes and committed to healing and restitution.

Moreover, historical adversity often highlights stories of resilience and unity that are particularly powerful. For example, the way communities have historically come together to rebuild after wars or natural disasters showcases the strength and solidarity of the human spirit. These narratives not only deepen national pride but also serve as blueprints for contemporary societal challenges, demonstrating the power of collective effort and mutual support.

In addition to formal histories, oral traditions and local stories also play a significant role in shaping the historical understanding of a nation. These narratives may not always find their place in mainstream history textbooks but are essential in preserving the experiences and wisdom of minority groups and local communities. They enrich the national historical narrative by providing a more comprehensive and diverse account of the past.

Education systems have a pivotal role in how history is conveyed to younger generations. By presenting a balanced view of history, educators can cultivate a well-rounded understanding of the past, highlighting both achievements and challenges. This educational approach helps students to develop critical thinking skills, enabling them to analyze historical events, understand different perspectives, and appreciate the complexity of historical narratives.

The media also plays a crucial role in how history is remembered and celebrated. Through documentaries, historical films, and media coverage of commemorative events, the media can bring historical stories to a wide audience, making history accessible and engaging. However, it is essential for such portrayals to be well-researched and respectful of historical accuracy to prevent the spread of misinformation and ensure that the lessons and pride derived from the past are based on truth.

As we reflect on the lessons from our history, it becomes apparent that pride in the past is not merely about glorifying what has been. It is about understanding the journey of a nation, learning from both its successes and its failures, and using these insights to forge a path forward that is informed by the past but oriented towards a hopeful and inclusive future.

· · ·

"Unity in diversity is not just a slogan; it's a blueprint for building a stronger nation. It's about celebrating the myriad threads that weave our national tapestry. Together, we are vibrant; divided, we are diminished."

• • •

CHAPTER III

Unity in Diversity: Celebrating Cultural Richness

The mosaic of a nation's identity is intricately pieced together with the varied hues of its cultural, ethnic, linguistic, and religious diversity. This diversity is not a mere backdrop to daily life but a vibrant and dynamic force that enriches society. Embracing and celebrating this diversity is not just about acknowledging differences but about understanding and leveraging these differences to foster national unity and collective strength.

Cultural richness can be seen in the myriad traditions, festivals, languages, and customs that populate a nation. Each cultural practice offers a window into the lives and histories of the people who carry them forward. For example, festivals, which often originate from religious or historical events, are celebrated with specific rituals, music, dance, and food, each element bearing significance and offering joy and cohesion among participants.

Language diversity is another profound aspect of cultural richness. Each language carries its own unique worldview, idioms, poetry, and philosophy. Efforts to preserve and promote indigenous and regional languages not only help protect these languages from extinction but also enrich the national linguistic landscape. Bilingual or multilingual policies in education and administration not only respect linguistic diversity but also enhance communication and understanding across different linguistic communities.

The culinary diversity found within a nation is a delicious testament to its cultural richness. The flavors, ingredients, and cooking methods used across different regions not only tantalize the palate but also tell stories of migration, trade, agricultural practices, and cultural exchange. Culinary festivals and food fairs can be significant in promoting national unity by bringing people together to share and celebrate their culinary traditions.

Art and literature are reflections of cultural identity and diversity. They are powerful mediums through which stories are told, histories are recounted, and societal values are critiqued and celebrated. Supporting a diverse array of artistic and literary expressions ensures that multiple perspectives are heard and valued. Art exhibitions, literary festivals, and public funding for arts can help promote these diverse voices and foster a culturally rich and inclusive public space.

Religious diversity is another cornerstone of cultural richness. Each religious community brings its own beliefs, practices, and celebrations to the national fabric. Interfaith dialogue and celebrations can promote understanding and respect among different religious groups. These interactions not only dispel misconceptions and reduce conflicts but also build bridges of cooperation that enhance societal harmony.

In addition to these cultural elements, traditional crafts and practices such as weaving, pottery, and folk music and dance are vital aspects of cultural heritage. Supporting these crafts through fairs, museums, and educational programs can provide economic benefits to local communities while preserving important cultural knowledge and skills.

Education systems that incorporate multicultural education frameworks play a crucial role in celebrating diversity. Schools that teach about different cultures, languages, and religions help cultivate respect and appreciation among young citizens. These educational experiences prepare students to navigate and thrive in a diverse society, equipping them with the skills to communicate across cultural boundaries and to challenge stereotypes and prejudices.

Media also has a significant role in promoting cultural diversity. By showcasing diverse cultural expressions and narratives, the media can help normalize diversity as a strength rather than a divider. Representation matters, and when people see their languages, cultures, and histories reflected in the media, they feel recognized and valued as part of the national narrative.

Celebrating cultural richness ultimately contributes to a stronger, more cohesive society. It fosters an environment where differences are not just tolerated but are embraced as sources of strength and innovation. In a world that is increasingly interconnected, the ability to engage with and appreciate diverse cultures is not just a national asset but a global necessity. Thus, by promoting unity in diversity, a nation not only enriches its own cultural landscape but also sets a global example of inclusivity and cooperation.

• • •

"Positive thinking in the realm of patriotism is a catalyst for change. It inspires us to overcome challenges not just with strength, but with grace and wisdom. Let this mindset be the wind that sails our national vessel forward."

• • •

CHAPTER IV

The Power of Positivity: Shaping Our National Mindset

Positivity is a powerful force that can transform individual lives and reshape entire societies. When cultivated at a national level, a positive mindset can enhance resilience, foster creativity, and strengthen community bonds, all of which are crucial for societal progress and cohesion. This chapter explores how positivity influences a nation's spirit and how it can be harnessed to create a more harmonious and forward-looking society.

At the heart of positivity is the ability to focus on opportunities rather than obstacles, which can significantly influence how a nation responds to challenges. A positive national mindset encourages resilience—citizens and leaders alike are more likely to view setbacks as temporary and surmountable. This outlook not only helps in recovering from crises but also in turning challenging situations into opportunities for growth and development.

Education plays a pivotal role in fostering a positive national mindset. Schools that incorporate positive psychology practices into their curriculum help students develop a growth mindset, where challenges are seen as opportunities to learn and improve. Teaching methodologies that focus on student strengths and potential rather than solely on correcting weaknesses can lead to higher levels of motivation and engagement among students. Moreover, educational content that highlights national achievements and constructive contributions to humanity can instill pride and optimism in young minds.

Media also has a significant impact on the national mindset. Positive news and stories that highlight human kindness, technological breakthroughs, and artistic achievements can inspire hope and encourage a focus on the positive aspects of life. Conversely, an overemphasis on negative news can lead to despair and a skewed perception of reality. Therefore, balanced media that showcases both challenges and successes is essential for maintaining a healthy national mindset.

Leadership is crucial in shaping a positive national mindset. Leaders who exhibit optimism, integrity, and compassion can inspire those qualities in their citizens. When leaders focus on unity, peace, and collective progress, they set a tone that resonates throughout the country. Political speeches, public engagements, and national policies that emphasize collaborative success and social harmony can significantly influence public sentiment and foster a spirit of national unity and positivity.

Community initiatives that promote social engagement and volunteerism also play a crucial role in cultivating positivity. When individuals engage in community service, they not only contribute to societal well-being but also enrich their own lives. These activities foster a sense of purpose and belonging, which are key components of a positive outlook. Community centers, local NGOs, and civic groups can facilitate such initiatives by organizing and promoting activities that address local needs and encourage community participation.

Health and wellness are also deeply connected to positivity. A nation that prioritizes public health, provides mental health support, and promotes physical wellness is more likely to foster a positive mindset among its citizens. Health programs that emphasize preventive care and holistic wellness contribute to a healthier, happier populace, which in turn is better equipped to contribute positively to society.

Cultural events and national celebrations are manifestations of a positive national spirit. These events often serve as platforms for expressing collective joy and pride. They not only bring people together but also reinforce national identity and the positive values associated with it. By celebrating cultural heritage, achievements, and national heroes, these events strengthen the bonds between citizens and enhance national unity.

Finally, fostering a positive national mindset is not just about promoting an idealistic view of the world. It involves recognizing and addressing real challenges while choosing to focus on solutions and improvements. It requires a collective effort across all sectors of society—government, education, media, businesses, and community organizations—to cultivate an environment that values optimism, resilience, and proactive engagement.

The power of positivity, when embedded in the national consciousness, can lead to transformative outcomes. It can turn adversity into progress, diversity into strength, and challenges into opportunities. By nurturing this mindset, a nation not only enhances its internal cohesion and resilience but also positions itself as a positive influence on the global stage.

• • •

"The power of an educated citizenry is the foundation of every successful nation. Education is not just about gaining knowledge; it's about building the character of our future leaders. Invest in education, and you invest in the future of our country."

• • •

CHAPTER V

Women at the Forefront: Female Leaders in National Development

The role of women in shaping national development is both profound and pivotal. As nations evolve, the inclusion of women in leadership roles across various sectors not only enhances societal progress but also ensures a more balanced and equitable approach to national development. This exploration into the contributions of female leaders provides insights into how their involvement has transformed societies and fostered sustainable growth.

Female leadership brings unique perspectives and strategies to the table, often emphasizing collaboration, inclusivity, and long-term solutions. The participation of women in politics, for instance, has led to more comprehensive policymaking that often includes robust considerations for health, education, family welfare, and social justice—areas that are crucial for holistic national development. Political leaders, such as prime ministers, presidents, and members of parliament, have shown that leadership styles characterized by empathy and inclusivity can result in more effective governance.

In the corporate sector, female executives and entrepreneurs have redefined business practices with innovative approaches and ethical leadership. Studies have shown that companies with women in top management roles often experience better financial performance and higher levels of creativity and innovation. This is attributed to their diverse perspectives and an inclusive approach to decision-making. Moreover, women leaders in business are more likely to advocate for sustainable practices and corporate social responsibility, aligning business goals with broader social and environmental concerns.

The impact of women in the fields of science and technology also cannot be understated. Female scientists, engineers, and technologists contribute significantly to innovation and research. By breaking barriers in these traditionally male-dominated fields, they inspire future generations of girls to pursue education and careers in STEM (science, technology, engineering, and mathematics), thereby promoting gender equality and strengthening the nation's intellectual and technological capital.

In the realm of education, women as educators and administrators play a critical role in shaping educational policies and practices. Their leadership in curriculum development, educational planning, and pedagogy has been pivotal in promoting more adaptive and inclusive education systems. Women in these roles often prioritize access to education for all, championing policies that reduce disparities and promote quality education across gender, social, and economic lines.

Cultural leadership is another area where women have made significant strides. Female artists, writers, filmmakers, and performers use their crafts to express cultural narratives and influence social norms. Through their work, they challenge stereotypes and advocate for social changes that lead to greater gender equality and broader societal reforms. Their creative contributions not only enrich the cultural landscape but also spark critical conversations about national identity, values, and the dynamics of power and gender.

Women's contributions to social movements and non-governmental organizations (NGOs) highlight their capability in leading social change. As advocates for human rights, environmental protection, and social justice, women have spearheaded initiatives that address some of the most pressing challenges facing their communities and nations. These leaders mobilize resources, create impactful campaigns, and drive legislative changes that improve the lives of millions.

In healthcare, women as medical professionals, researchers, and policymakers are indispensable. Their efforts in improving healthcare accessibility, advancing medical research, and implementing public health initiatives have saved countless lives and improved the wellbeing of entire populations. Women in healthcare leadership positions ensure that health systems are responsive to the needs of all segments of society, including the most vulnerable.

The journey of women to these forefronts of national development has not been without challenges. Gender biases, societal norms, and institutional barriers have often impeded their progress. Recognizing and addressing these barriers is essential for any nation that seeks to benefit fully from the capabilities of all its citizens. Policies that support gender equality, such as equal pay, parental leave, and anti-discrimination laws, are crucial in leveling the playing field.

As we continue to witness the rising influence of female leaders across all sectors of society, it is clear that their involvement is not just beneficial but essential for sustainable and inclusive development. The unique perspectives and leadership styles of women, characterized by empathy, inclusiveness, and resilience, contribute significantly to the social, economic, and political fabric of a nation. Encouraging and facilitating more women to take on leadership roles is a testament to a nation's commitment to gender equality and its overall development.

• • •

"Every artist dips their brush into their soul, painting their nation's story with strokes of heritage and hues of unity. Art is not just expression; it is a dialogue of generations, a narrative of its people's spirit. Let us cherish and foster this artistic dialogue."

• • •

CHAPTER VI

Youth and Patriotism: Engaging the Next Generation

The engagement of young people is crucial for the sustenance and growth of patriotic sentiments within a nation. As bearers of future responsibilities, the youth shape and redefine national identity through their energy, innovation, and vision. Effective engagement with this dynamic demographic not only fosters a deep sense of national pride but also ensures the continuity of these values through generations.

Education systems play a fundamental role in cultivating patriotism among young people. Schools and universities are not just centers for academic learning but also arenas where young minds are introduced to national history, symbols, and values. Curricula that incorporate comprehensive national history, civic responsibilities, and the rights of citizens help students understand the importance of their role in national development. Moreover, educational programs that include discussions about national heroes, significant national events, and key democratic principles can inspire pride and a sense of belonging among students.

Youth organizations and extracurricular activities also provide platforms for expressing and nurturing patriotism. Activities such as community service, participation in national celebrations, and involvement in local governance can immerse young individuals in the practical aspects of civic engagement. These experiences not only instill a sense of duty and community but also allow young people to see firsthand the impact of their contributions to society.

The role of digital media is increasingly significant in engaging the youth. In today's digital age, social media platforms, online forums, and multimedia resources serve as important tools for spreading patriotic messages and engaging discussions about national identity and civic responsibilities. By leveraging these platforms, educators, leaders, and policymakers can reach out to the youth in spaces that are familiar to them, presenting patriotism in a context that resonates with their daily lives and interests.

Moreover, the involvement of young people in policy-making and national affairs is essential for fostering patriotism. When young individuals are included in discussions about national issues, they are more likely to feel valued and responsible for the outcomes of these discussions. Platforms such as youth parliaments, advisory boards, and consultation groups can provide opportunities for young citizens to voice their opinions and learn about governance processes, thereby deepening their commitment to national interests and their understanding of the complexities of leadership and decision-making.

Cultural exchanges and international youth programs further broaden the perspectives of young people and reinforce their appreciation for their own national heritage. Exposure to different cultures promotes a deeper understanding of global interdependencies and the unique position of one's own nation in the global community. Such programs not only cultivate a sense of national pride but also encourage a form of patriotism that acknowledges and respects global diversity.

Celebrating national achievements in areas such as sports, arts, and science can be particularly appealing to the youth. National athletes, artists, and scientists serve as role models, demonstrating the heights that can be achieved through dedication and talent. Supporting and publicizing these achievements can inspire young people to excel and contribute to the national legacy in their own unique ways.

Challenges to patriotism, such as political disillusionment and global conflicts, require that young people be equipped with critical thinking skills to analyze and respond to such issues. Education that encourages open dialogue about national shortcomings and global issues can prepare the youth to handle these challenges with insight and balance. It is important that the discourse around patriotism avoids blind nationalism and instead promotes a reflective and inclusive form of national pride.

Ultimately, engaging the next generation in the discourse of patriotism necessitates a multi-faceted approach that combines education, media, participatory governance, and cultural exchanges. By creating opportunities for the youth to learn about, experience, and contribute to their nation, societies can cultivate a form of patriotism that is both informed and impassioned. This approach ensures that as these young individuals grow, their patriotism matures into a committed and constructive force that positively influences their nation's path towards progress and unity.

• • •

"Technology bridges distances and knits the nation closer, turning our diversity into our strength. In every byte and pixel, there lies an opportunity to connect and collaborate. Let's harness this digital frontier for the unity of our land."

- - -

CHAPTER VII

Symbols of Pride: National Symbols and Their Meanings

National symbols are powerful emblems that encapsulate the history, culture, and values of a nation. They serve as points of pride and unity, providing a visual and often emotional connection to the nation's heritage and identity. These symbols can vary widely—from flags and national anthems to monuments and natural landmarks—each carrying deep significance and helping to reinforce national unity among diverse populations.

The national flag is perhaps the most universally recognized symbol of national identity. Typically, each color and element on a flag has specific meanings associated with the country's history or natural features. For example, the colors might represent the nation's landscape, such as blue for the ocean or green for the land, while symbols like stars or stripes can represent historical events or the structure of the country. The flag is not merely a piece of cloth but a reminder of the nation's journey, its battles, and its victories. It evokes feelings of loyalty and pride in the citizens and is prominently displayed during national holidays and significant events.

The national anthem is another potent symbol, embodying the spirit, struggles, and aspirations of a nation through its lyrics and melody. An anthem can narrate the story of a nation's resilience, celebrate its freedom, or honor its heroes. When played or sung, it commands respect and evokes a collective sense of identity and belonging among its citizens, often stirring deep emotions and patriotism.

Monuments and memorials play a crucial role in symbolizing national heritage and honoring important figures and events in a nation's history. These structures serve as tangible reminders of the past, offering a place for reflection, commemoration, and education. They also act as focal points for national ceremonies, providing spaces where people can come together to celebrate achievements or remember sacrifices made for the country's sake.

Natural landmarks such as rivers, mountains, and forests can also serve as national symbols. These natural features often hold cultural significance and are linked to historical events or indigenous stories. They not only contribute to national identity but also remind citizens of their nation's beauty and ecological wealth. Efforts to conserve these landmarks reflect the values of respect and stewardship that are central to the nation's ethos.

Cultural symbols, including traditional attire, crafts, dances, and festivals, also play a significant role in defining a nation's identity. These symbols are often rooted in the nation's historical and social fabric, representing the unique ways of life and artistic expressions of different communities within the nation. By celebrating these cultural symbols through national events and educational programs, a nation can promote cultural diversity and inclusivity, reinforcing a broader, more cohesive national identity.

Language itself can be a powerful national symbol. A national language or languages often serve as a cornerstone of national policy and identity. It is not only a means of communication but also a repository of a community's collective memory, holding proverbs, poetry, literature, and historical documents. Efforts to promote and preserve national languages can strengthen a sense of unity and continuity with the past.

The use of national symbols in education is vital in imparting the values they represent to younger generations. Schools can integrate discussions of these symbols into the curriculum through history and social studies, helping students understand their historical contexts and contemporary relevance. This education fosters a deeper connection with the nation and its values from a young age.

Moreover, during international events, such as sports or cultural festivals, national symbols help represent a country on the global stage, fostering a sense of pride and unity among its citizens. They also facilitate cultural exchange and mutual understanding among nations, showcasing the uniqueness of each country and its culture.

National symbols are not just icons of statehood but are integral to the fabric of national identity. They are tools for education, reminders of history, and sources of pride and unity. Through these symbols, a nation communicates its values, celebrates its achievements, and honors its heritage. Maintaining respect for and knowledge of these symbols is essential for fostering a cohesive and patriotic society, where the past informs the present and inspires the future.

• • •

"*Economic empowerment leads to national prosperity but it starts with every individual's opportunity to thrive. When we lift up the least among us, we elevate the entire nation. It's about growth, not just in terms of wealth, but in spirit and equity.*"

* * *

CHAPTER VIII

Voices of Change: Stories of Inspirational National Figures

National figures who have made significant impacts on their societies are not just historical icons; they are embodiments of ideals, aspirations, and the relentless pursuit of change. Their stories inspire generations, motivating individuals and shaping national consciousness. These leaders, thinkers, and heroes come from various fields such as politics, science, arts, and social activism, each contributing uniquely to the narrative of their nation.

In politics, figures who have led movements for independence, democracy, or social reform are often revered. Their leadership during critical periods in a nation's history, whether in gaining independence or reforming governmental structures, demonstrates courage and vision. For instance, leaders who fought against colonial oppression or led significant reforms in democratic governance provide templates of bravery and service. Their speeches, writings, and actions continue to inspire political engagement and patriotism among citizens.

Scientific pioneers from a nation contribute not only through their inventions or discoveries but also through their dedication to pushing the boundaries of human knowledge. These individuals often overcome significant challenges, including limited resources and institutional support, to contribute to their fields. Their stories are potent reminders of the power of curiosity and resilience. Educators can use these narratives to spark interest in science and research among young students, illustrating how perseverance can lead to groundbreaking achievements.

Artistic figures such as poets, musicians, painters, and writers capture and express the cultural and emotional essence of their times. Their works often reflect societal values, struggles, and hopes. By engaging with these artistic expressions, citizens can experience a shared sense of identity and continuity with their cultural heritage. Celebrating these figures during national festivals or through educational curricula can strengthen appreciation for the arts and inspire new generations of artists.

Social activists are particularly impactful as national figures because they challenge the status quo and advocate for change. These individuals fight for rights, justice, and equality, often at great personal risk. Their courage to stand up for marginalized communities and to address systemic issues is deeply inspirational. Stories of such activists are powerful tools in educating the public about the importance of social justice and civic responsibility.

In addition to these well-known arenas, inspirational figures also emerge from less visible sectors such as sports, business, and community service. Athletes who excel in international competitions bring pride to their nations and often come to symbolize national strengths and aspirations. Entrepreneurs who innovate or contribute significantly to the economy demonstrate the potential of ingenuity and hard work. Community leaders who make substantial local changes through grassroots initiatives show that significant impacts often start at the local level.

The stories of these national figures are shared through various media, including films, books, documentaries, and educational programs. These narratives not only preserve the memory of these individuals but also make their lives accessible to a broader audience. Schools can incorporate these stories into their curricula to teach values such as perseverance, integrity, and compassion. Museums and memorials dedicated to these figures serve as spaces for reflection and learning.

Moreover, the stories of national figures hold particular resonance during times of national crisis or celebration. In moments of challenge, these stories remind citizens of their shared heritage of resilience and innovation. During celebrations, they serve as sources of communal pride and joy. By evoking a sense of common purpose and identity, these stories can unify a nation around shared values and goals.

It is important for contemporary leaders and educators to continue recognizing and promoting the stories of inspirational figures. By doing so, they ensure that the lessons of the past are not forgotten and that new generations are motivated to contribute positively to their society. The narratives of past and present national figures are not just tales of individual accomplishment but are collective assets that can inspire and mobilize a nation towards greater unity and achievement. Through these stories, a nation finds its voice, its values, and its vision for the future.

• • •

"Environmental patriotism is our shared responsibility to treasure and protect the natural wealth of our nation. Our land's beauty is its heritage; preserving this treasure is a testament to our love for our country. Let every tree planted, and every river cleaned, be a pledge of our dedication."

• • •

CHAPTER IX

Education for Empowerment: Teaching Patriotism in Schools

Education plays a critical role in shaping the minds and values of young people, making it a pivotal arena for instilling a sense of national pride and responsibility. Teaching patriotism in schools involves more than just recounting historical facts; it encompasses fostering a deep understanding and appreciation for the nation's heritage, democratic principles, and civic responsibilities.

This comprehensive approach ensures that students not only feel proud of their country but are also prepared to contribute positively to its development and uphold its values.

At the core of patriotic education is the development of a well-rounded understanding of the nation's history. This includes both its triumphs and trials, providing students with a nuanced perspective of their country's journey.

Lessons that detail the struggles for independence, the formation of the constitution, and significant reform movements help students appreciate the sacrifices made by their forebears and understand the hard-earned nature of their freedoms. This historical awareness fosters a sense of continuity with the past and a responsibility to maintain and build upon the legacy received.

Civic education is another crucial element of teaching patriotism. By understanding the workings of government, the rights and responsibilities of citizens, and the importance of laws and governance, students are equipped to participate effectively and responsibly in their nation.

Civic education should also involve practical experiences such as visits to local government institutions, participation in student councils, and engagement in community service. These activities provide hands-on learning about the importance of involvement in civic life and the impact one can have on community and country.

The integration of patriotic songs, symbols, and rituals in school activities also plays a significant role in fostering patriotism. National anthems, flags, and pledges, when understood and respected, can evoke a sense of pride and unity among students. Celebrations of national holidays and anniversaries of significant historical events can further enhance this connection, making patriotism a lived experience rather than just a concept.

Moreover, the inclusion of literature and arts that reflect the nation's cultural heritage in the curriculum can deepen students' connection to their country. Stories, poems, paintings, and performances that explore national themes or are created by compatriots can be powerful in cultivating a sense of national pride and identity. These cultural elements not only enhance the appreciation of the nation's artistic legacy but also help students understand diverse perspectives and experiences within their country, promoting a more inclusive form of patriotism.

Discussion and debate about national issues should also be encouraged within the educational framework. This fosters critical thinking and allows students to engage actively with current events and challenges facing their country.

Such discussions should be conducted in a manner that respects differing viewpoints and encourages constructive dialogue. By learning to engage in respectful and informed discussions, students can better understand the complexities of national and global issues and their role in addressing them.

Another important aspect of teaching patriotism in schools is acknowledging and celebrating the country's diversity. This includes recognizing the contributions of various ethnic, cultural, and religious groups to the nation's development. Such recognition not only promotes a more inclusive view of the nation's history but also underscores the strength that lies in diversity.

It helps young people appreciate the different backgrounds and traditions that coexist in their country, fostering a sense of unity and shared destiny.

In addition to formal education, extracurricular activities such as sports, music bands, and clubs can also promote patriotic education. These groups often bring students together across different backgrounds for a common goal, fostering teamwork, discipline, and a sense of community—qualities that are essential for a strong and cohesive nation.

Finally, the role of educators in teaching patriotism cannot be overstated. Teachers who model respect, integrity, and civic-mindedness can profoundly influence their students' attitudes and values. Professional development opportunities that help educators effectively teach patriotism and civic engagement are crucial for ensuring that this education is impactful and meaningful.

Teaching patriotism in schools is a multifaceted endeavor that requires a thoughtful and comprehensive approach. By combining history and civic education with cultural studies and practical experiences, schools can nurture well-informed, responsible citizens who are proud of their heritage and committed to contributing positively to their nation's future.

• • •

"The stories of our national heroes are the echoes of our nation's heartbeats. They teach us resilience, sacrifice, and the undying hope for a better tomorrow. Let us carry their legacy forward with honor and action."

• • •

CHAPTER X

Community Spirit: Building Bonds at the Local Level

The essence of a strong nation lies in the strength and vitality of its communities. Community spirit, the collective sense of commitment and connection among local residents, is fundamental to building resilient, supportive, and cohesive local environments. This spirit is nurtured through shared experiences, collective participation in local affairs, and the fostering of mutual respect and understanding among diverse groups. By strengthening bonds at the local level, communities can contribute significantly to broader national unity and solidarity.

One of the key strategies for building community spirit is encouraging active participation in local governance and decision-making processes. When residents feel they have a voice in local affairs, they are more likely to engage actively and contribute positively to their communities. This can be facilitated through town hall meetings, local councils, and public forums where community members can express their views, raise concerns, and offer solutions. Such participatory approaches help residents feel connected to their local government and empower them to take part in shaping the future of their community.

Community events and festivals play a crucial role in building local bonds. These gatherings, whether centered around cultural, religious, or seasonal themes, provide opportunities for residents to celebrate shared traditions and create new memories. Events like local fairs, sports tournaments, music concerts, and holiday celebrations can draw diverse groups together, promoting a sense of belonging and shared identity. These events also offer a platform for showcasing local talents and crafts, further enriching the community's cultural landscape.

Volunteerism is another powerful tool for strengthening community spirit. By engaging in volunteer activities, residents can address local needs and challenges collaboratively. Initiatives such as neighborhood clean-ups, food drives, tutoring programs, and elder care support not only improve community welfare but also build a culture of mutual assistance and empathy. Such activities can foster a sense of pride and investment in the local area, reinforcing the bonds among residents.

Local education initiatives can also contribute to community spirit. Schools are not just places for academic learning; they are hubs of community activity that can bring together families, educators, and local businesses. Programs that involve parents and local residents in school activities, such as reading days, art shows, and science fairs, encourage broader community engagement with local education. Schools can also promote community spirit by teaching students about local history and heritage, thus instilling a sense of pride and belonging from a young age.

Community centers serve as vital spaces for fostering local bonds. These centers can offer a range of activities and services that cater to various interests and age groups, such as sports leagues, art classes, social clubs, and educational workshops. By providing a common space for residents to gather, learn, and entertain, community centers help cultivate a sense of togetherness and serve as a resource for personal and communal growth.

The inclusion of diverse community voices is essential for building a strong community spirit. Efforts should be made to ensure that all groups, including minorities, immigrants, and other marginalized populations, are represented and have opportunities to contribute to community life. This can be achieved through inclusive policies and practices that respect and celebrate diversity, such as multicultural events, translation services at public meetings, and diverse representation in community organizations.

Local media also plays a significant role in nurturing community spirit. Local newspapers, radio stations, and social media platforms can highlight community successes, announce upcoming events, and celebrate local heroes. By focusing on positive stories and community achievements, local media can help foster a positive community image and encourage greater civic pride and participation.

Building community spirit is a multifaceted endeavor that requires the collaboration of various stakeholders, including local governments, organizations, schools, and residents. Through active participation, celebratory events, volunteerism, educational initiatives, and inclusive practices, communities can strengthen their internal bonds and contribute to the overall health and unity of the nation. By nurturing these local connections, communities not only enhance the quality of life for their residents but also lay the groundwork for a cohesive and resilient society.

• • •

"Volunteerism is the ultimate expression of democracy, empowering individuals to act and inspire change. It is through service to others that we truly understand the meaning of community and nationhood. Let's give back, not out of obligation, but out of gratitude."

. . .

CHAPTER XI

The Role of Media: Promoting Positive Narratives

The media plays a transformative role in shaping public opinion and cultural norms. Its capacity to reach wide audiences quickly and effectively makes it a powerful tool in promoting positive narratives that can inspire, educate, and unite. In the context of national development and social cohesion, the media's responsibility extends beyond mere reporting—it involves curating content that fosters understanding, highlights progress, and builds a sense of shared identity among the populace.

One of the primary ways media can promote positive narratives is by focusing on stories of success and resilience within the community. Coverage of local heroes, successful community projects, advancements in science and technology, or significant achievements in sports and arts can instill a sense of pride and optimism. These stories not only serve as a source of inspiration but also demonstrate the potential for success and the positive impact of perseverance and hard work. By celebrating these achievements, the media can motivate individuals and communities to strive for excellence and engage in positive activities.

Moreover, the media has the ability to educate the public on important issues by providing accurate, balanced, and insightful information. Educational programming, documentaries, and in-depth analysis of current events can help people understand complex issues and the impact of policies on their lives and society at large. This type of content encourages informed citizenship and promotes a culture of learning and inquiry that is essential for a healthy democracy.

The media also plays a crucial role in shaping perceptions of national identity and unity. By highlighting stories that showcase cultural diversity and the successful integration of different communities, the media can promote a more inclusive national narrative. Coverage that respects and celebrates diversity while focusing on common values and goals can help bridge cultural and social divides, fostering unity and mutual respect among various groups.

In addition to traditional news, the media can utilize entertainment to convey positive messages and values. Films, television shows, and online content that incorporate themes of teamwork, justice, integrity, and community service can subtly influence public attitudes and behavior. Entertainment media that highlights ethical dilemmas and moral victories can serve as a catalyst for public discussion and personal reflection, reinforcing societal norms and values.

The role of media in crisis situations is particularly critical. During natural disasters, pandemics, or social unrest, the media's role in disseminating vital information and uplifting stories is paramount. Responsible reporting that focuses on relief efforts, heroic acts, and community solidarity rather than just the sensational aspects of the crisis can help maintain public morale and encourage active participation in recovery efforts.

Social media, with its widespread use and immediate impact, offers an additional platform for promoting positive narratives. Individuals and organizations can use these platforms to share positive content, engage with the community, and mobilize support for beneficial causes. However, the potential for misinformation on social media makes it essential for users to maintain diligence and seek out reliable sources of information.

The media also has a responsibility to engage in self-reflection and strive for high ethical standards. This includes ensuring that their content does not perpetuate stereotypes, incite violence, or spread misinformation. Training programs for journalists and media professionals on ethical reporting, cultural sensitivity, and fact-checking are crucial for maintaining the integrity of the media.

The media's role in promoting positive narratives is multifaceted and profoundly influential. Through responsible reporting, educational content, inclusive storytelling, and ethical practices, the media can help cultivate a well-informed, unified, and optimistic society. By choosing to highlight the best of humanity and the potential for positive change, the media not only informs but also inspires, playing a crucial role in the progress and cohesion of any nation.

• • •

"In the symphony of a great nation, every citizen's voice matters. It's in the diversity of these voices that a nation finds its true harmony. Let's cherish and amplify every voice, for in each lies the unique melody of our homeland."

• • •

CHAPTER XII

Arts and Patriotism: Expressing Love for the Country Through Art

Art has long been a profound medium for expressing national pride and patriotism. Through various forms such as painting, sculpture, music, literature, and performance, artists have captured the essence of their countries' histories, landscapes, people, and ideologies. Art not only reflects a nation's culture but also reinforces and reshapes the collective memory and identity of its people. It serves as a powerful tool for fostering national unity, invoking reflection, and sometimes provoking necessary social change.

Visual arts, including painting and sculpture, have historically played significant roles in celebrating national themes. Artists use their canvases and materials to depict significant historical events, national heroes, and beautiful landscapes that symbolize their homeland's pride. These artworks often become iconic symbols of national identity and are cherished as national treasures. Museums and galleries that house these works provide spaces where citizens can connect with their country's heritage and appreciate the collective journey of their people.

Literature is another potent vessel for patriotic expression. Writers encapsulate the spirit of their times, weaving narratives that reflect societal values, struggles, and triumphs. Through poetry, novels, and plays, authors explore themes of freedom, justice, and national identity. Literature allows readers to delve into the emotional and ideological depths of their national heritage and encourages them to reflect on their role within their nation. Celebrated works often become part of a nation's educational curriculum, ensuring that each generation connects with its national heritage through these literary expressions.

Music and patriotic songs play an undeniable role in fostering national unity and pride. National anthems are perhaps the most direct expressions of patriotism, played at official events and sports games to inspire solidarity and honor the country. Beyond anthems, many composers and musicians create works that evoke the nation's landscape, history, and folklore. These compositions can unite listeners under a common sentiment of nostalgia, pride, and love for their homeland.

Performance arts such as theater, dance, and cinema also contribute significantly to patriotic expression. These mediums combine elements of storytelling, music, and visual cues to create compelling narratives that celebrate national history or critique its shortcomings. Performances can be particularly powerful in conveying patriotic themes because they are live and interactive, engaging audiences in a shared, communal experience. Festivals, public performances, and national celebrations often feature such artistic expressions, reinforcing national values and fostering a sense of community among participants.

Furthermore, the digital arts and new media have opened up innovative avenues for expressing patriotism. Digital artists utilize technology to create multimedia experiences that can reach a broader audience through the internet. Video games, digital installations, and virtual reality experiences can also communicate patriotic themes in ways that are interactive and immersive, appealing particularly to the younger generation.

The inclusion of diverse artistic voices is crucial in the representation of a nation's patriotism. A country is made up of individuals from various backgrounds, and each group may have different ways of expressing their national pride. Inclusive artistic expression that acknowledges and celebrates this diversity can lead to a richer, more comprehensive understanding of what it means to love and belong to a nation. It can also help to address and heal historical or social divisions by bringing to light different perspectives within the national narrative.

Artists often play the role of social commentators, using their works to not only celebrate but also critically examine their nations' policies, cultures, and histories. Through their creative expressions, they can challenge the status quo and inspire discussions about national identity, values, and the path forward. This critical engagement is essential for a dynamic and evolving patriotic sentiment that does not merely celebrate the past but also anticipates the future.

Art in its myriad forms serves as a profound channel for expressing and shaping patriotism. Whether through traditional media like painting and literature or through contemporary forms like digital art and multimedia, artistic expressions continue to inspire, unite, and provoke reflection among the citizens of a nation. By engaging with art, individuals can connect more deeply with their country's past, present, and future, fostering a sense of pride and responsibility that transcends generations.

• • •

"To overcome divisions, we must build bridges of empathy and understanding across our differences. It is through our shared struggles and collective triumphs that we forge a united path forward. This journey isn't about erasing our differences but embracing them."

. . .

CHAPTER XIII

Technology for Unity: Digital Tools that Bring Us Together

In the contemporary world, technology plays an indispensable role in fostering unity and connectivity among people. Digital tools and platforms have transformed how individuals and communities interact, collaborate, and engage with each other, breaking down traditional barriers of distance and time. This capability to connect broadly and efficiently makes technology a powerful enabler of unity, providing innovative ways to promote inclusion, participation, and shared experiences across a nation.

One of the most significant contributions of technology to unity is through the realm of communication. Social media platforms, instant messaging apps, and video conferencing tools have redefined the way people communicate. These technologies allow individuals to maintain relationships over long distances, participate in community discussions, share experiences, and express their opinions freely. Such interactions can foster a sense of belonging and community among users, linking people from various parts of a country or even expatriates with their homeland.

Moreover, digital platforms facilitate the organization and mobilization of community and national events that foster unity. Online forums and social media can be used to organize gatherings, protests, celebrations, and charity events, encouraging widespread participation. The ease and low cost of digital organization tools democratize the ability to mobilize people for causes, allowing grassroots movements and community initiatives to gain traction and visibility quickly.

Education technology (EdTech) is another powerful unifier. Online learning platforms, virtual classrooms, and educational apps provide access to quality education regardless of geographical location. This accessibility is particularly important in bridging the urban-rural divide, ensuring that remote areas are not left behind in educational opportunities. Through shared educational experiences and resources, a collective level of knowledge and a common base of information are established, contributing to a more informed and cohesive society.

Digital governance and e-governance platforms significantly contribute to national unity by making government services accessible to all citizens, enhancing transparency, and ensuring equitable distribution of resources. Services such as online tax filing, registration of births and deaths, passport services, and social welfare programs that are accessible via the internet can save time and reduce physical barriers to accessing government assistance. Such inclusivity fosters trust and participation in the governmental process, crucial components of a unified nation.

Healthcare technology also plays a vital role in unifying a nation by improving access to medical services. Telemedicine platforms, mobile health apps, and online health resources can provide crucial healthcare services to underserved or remote areas, ensuring that all citizens have access to healthcare advice and support. This not only improves the overall health of the population but also promotes a sense of national well-being and solidarity.

In the realm of economic development, technology platforms like e-commerce and mobile banking empower individuals and small businesses by providing them access to national and global markets. These tools offer opportunities for economic growth and financial inclusion, helping to level the playing field for small enterprises and rural entrepreneurs. Economic empowerment through technology leads to a more balanced economic development across different regions of the country, fostering economic unity.

Public safety and emergency response technologies further demonstrate how digital tools can bring people together in times of need. Systems for early warning, crisis management, and community alerts can coordinate efforts during natural disasters or emergencies, enhancing the resilience of communities and fostering a spirit of cooperation and mutual aid.

Furthermore, technology can help preserve cultural heritage and promote national pride through digital archives, virtual tours of historical sites, and online exhibitions of traditional art and crafts. These resources make a nation's cultural heritage accessible to all, educating citizens about their history and promoting a shared sense of pride and identity.

Technology's role in promoting unity is multifaceted and profound. From improving communication and facilitating education to enhancing public services and economic opportunities, digital tools have the potential to unite people across geographical, social, and economic divides. As technology continues to evolve, it will undoubtedly play an increasingly central role in building a more connected, inclusive, and unified society. By harnessing the power of digital tools, nations can foster a sense of community and shared purpose among their citizens, paving the way for a cohesive and prosperous future.

• • •

"Celebrations of national holidays are the bookmarks in our nation's ongoing story. They remind us of our past struggles and achievements, and they reinvigorate our spirits for the challenges ahead. Let these days not just be of rest, but of reflection and rejuvenation."

• • •

CHAPTER XIV

Environmental Patriotism: Protecting Our Land

Environmental patriotism is a compelling blend of national pride and ecological responsibility, emphasizing the protection and preservation of a nation's natural resources as a core patriotic duty. This concept extends beyond mere conservation; it involves a deep-seated commitment to stewarding the environment as an integral part of a country's heritage and legacy for future generations. By nurturing a landscape that has sustained cultural, historical, and economic activities, citizens demonstrate their loyalty and love for their country through environmental action.

The foundation of environmental patriotism lies in the recognition of the intrinsic value of the natural world, which includes diverse ecosystems, wildlife, and natural landscapes. These are not only critical for the ecological balance and biodiversity but are also central to national identity and cultural heritage. Mountains, rivers, forests, and coastlines are often symbols of national pride and are celebrated in literature, folklore, and media. Preserving these natural features means maintaining part of the nation's soul and history.

Education plays a pivotal role in fostering environmental patriotism. Schools and educational institutions can integrate environmental education into their curricula, emphasizing the importance of sustainable practices and the impacts of environmental degradation. By educating students about local and global environmental issues, and the specific challenges faced by their own country, educators can cultivate a sense of responsibility and duty to protect their natural surroundings. Educational initiatives can also include practical activities such as tree planting, recycling projects, and field trips to natural reserves, which not only teach students about the environment but also engage them in protective actions.

Community involvement is crucial in environmental conservation efforts. Local communities are often the first to experience the benefits of a healthy environment and the first to suffer from its degradation. Community-led initiatives, such as local clean-up days, conservation projects, and wildlife protection programs, can empower citizens to take an active role in preserving their surroundings. Moreover, these activities strengthen community bonds and reinforce a collective identity rooted in a shared environment.

Government policies and regulations also play a significant role in fostering environmental patriotism by setting standards and goals for conservation, pollution control, and sustainable development. These can include laws protecting endangered species, regulations limiting pollution, incentives for renewable energy use, and penalties for environmental violations. By implementing and enforcing these policies, governments demonstrate their commitment to protecting the nation's natural heritage and encourage citizens to adopt environmentally friendly practices.

Media and public awareness campaigns are powerful tools for promoting environmental patriotism. By highlighting the beauty of the nation's landscapes and the threats they face, media can inspire a sense of urgency and responsibility among the populace. Documentaries, articles, and social media content that showcase successful conservation efforts can serve as inspiration for similar actions by individuals and groups. These campaigns can also educate the public about the simple steps everyone can take to reduce their environmental footprint, such as reducing waste, conserving water, and supporting sustainable products.

Businesses and corporations can contribute to environmental patriotism by adopting green practices and supporting environmental initiatives. This can include reducing emissions, using sustainable materials, and investing in community conservation projects. By demonstrating their commitment to environmental stewardship, businesses not only contribute to the preservation of the national environment but also build goodwill among consumers who value ecological responsibility.

International cooperation is another dimension of environmental patriotism. As environmental issues often transcend national borders, collaborating with other nations on issues such as climate change, biodiversity conservation, and pollution control can enhance a country's own efforts to protect its environment. This cooperation can be seen in the participation in international agreements and collaborations on environmental projects.

Environmental patriotism is a multifaceted approach to national pride and responsibility. It encompasses educational initiatives, community action, government policies, media involvement, corporate responsibility, and international cooperation, all aimed at protecting and preserving the natural environment. By embracing environmental patriotism, citizens demonstrate their love and duty to their country not only in the present but also in securing a sustainable and prosperous future for generations to come.

• • •

"The role of media in shaping the narrative of a nation is undeniable. It has the power to divide or unite through the stories it chooses to tell. Let us advocate for media that uplifts, educates, and unites."

• • •

CHAPTER XV

Celebrations of Unity: National Holidays and Their Significance

National holidays are pivotal in fostering a sense of unity and shared identity among the citizens of a country. These days are set aside to celebrate significant historical events, honor national heroes, and reflect on the nation's heritage and values. Through parades, ceremonies, and public gatherings, national holidays provide an opportunity for collective reflection, celebration, and patriotism. They serve as reminders of a nation's journey, its trials, triumphs, and the common values that bind its people together.

One of the primary functions of national holidays is to commemorate important moments in a nation's history. Whether it is the anniversary of independence, the signing of a peace treaty, or a major military victory, these holidays serve as a reminder of the milestones that have shaped the country. They offer a chance for citizens to reflect on their past, the struggles their forebearers endured, and the achievements that have been made. This reflection not only deepens an understanding of national history but also reinforces the lessons learned and the values upheld during those pivotal times.

Moreover, national holidays are significant in honoring the individuals who have played crucial roles in the nation's history. Heroes and leaders who fought for freedom, justice, and human rights are often commemorated during these celebrations. By remembering their contributions, citizens are reminded of the virtues of courage, sacrifice, and leadership. Memorials and educational events held on these days can also serve to educate the younger generations about these figures, ensuring that the legacy of these leaders continues to inspire future citizens.

In addition to their commemorative function, national holidays also serve as important tools for strengthening national unity and pride. Through various festive activities and symbols, such as flags, anthems, and military displays, these holidays cultivate a sense of common identity and shared purpose. They are times when differences are set aside, and individuals come together to celebrate the essence of their nationhood. This unity is further reinforced by the participation of various groups from different backgrounds, illustrating the diversity and inclusivity of the national community.

Public celebrations and parades during national holidays are significant in that they transform individual sentiment into a collective experience. These public gatherings are vibrant displays of national culture and heritage, featuring traditional music, dance, and cuisine. They provide a space for citizens to engage with one another in a festive atmosphere, promoting social cohesion and a sense of belonging. The inclusivity of these events, often involving various ethnic and social groups, helps to bridge societal gaps and promote mutual respect and understanding.

National holidays also play a crucial role in civic education. Schools and public institutions often organize events and activities that teach the importance of these holidays. Educational programs are designed to impart knowledge about the historical, cultural, and social significance of the events being commemorated. Through plays, recitals, and readings, children and young adults learn about their heritage and the responsibilities that come with citizenship.

Furthermore, these holidays can stimulate economic activity as they often involve public spending on decorations, events, and security. Local businesses and vendors also benefit from the increased public presence during parades and events. This economic aspect, while secondary, contributes to the national economy and can be seen as another way these celebrations benefit the country as a whole.

Another important aspect of national holidays is their role in international relations. These occasions often draw attention from other nations, and the presence of international dignitaries at celebrations can strengthen diplomatic ties. The way a country presents its history and values during these holidays can influence its global image and foster international goodwill.

National holidays are much more than public vacations or historical commemorations; they are profound opportunities for unity and reflection. They remind citizens of their shared past, celebrate their present achievements, and encourage a collective aspiration for the future. By bringing together people from all walks of life, these holidays reinforce national identity and promote a cohesive society, essential for any nation's ongoing harmony and prosperity.

• • •

"Cultural diplomacy is not merely about showcasing our diversity but about sharing our stories with the world. It's through these stories that we find common ground with others. Let's be ambassadors of our culture, in all its richness and variety."

• • •

CHAPTER XVI

Volunteerism and Service: Giving Back to the Nation

Volunteerism and community service are powerful expressions of civic responsibility and patriotism. By dedicating their time, skills, and resources, volunteers play a crucial role in strengthening their communities and, by extension, their nation. This commitment to service not only addresses immediate social needs but also fosters a culture of cooperation, altruism, and social cohesion. These activities are vital in building resilient communities that are capable of facing social, economic, and environmental challenges together.

The benefits of volunteerism extend well beyond the immediate assistance provided to individuals or communities. By engaging in volunteer activities, individuals develop a deeper understanding of the societal issues at play and gain a greater appreciation for the diversity and needs of their fellow citizens. This enhanced social awareness encourages a more informed and empathetic citizenry, capable of making thoughtful decisions about their community and country.

One of the most significant impacts of volunteerism is its ability to bridge gaps between diverse social groups. In many countries, social, economic, and cultural divisions can lead to misunderstandings and conflicts. Volunteer projects bring together people from different backgrounds, working towards a common goal, facilitating understanding and unity. These projects can be particularly transformative for young people, offering them opportunities to interact with others whose lives might be quite different from their own.

Volunteer activities also play a critical role in disaster response and recovery efforts. In times of crisis, such as natural disasters or national emergencies, volunteers are often on the front lines, providing essential aid and support to affected populations. Their quick mobilization and selfless service can be critical to saving lives and restoring communities. Moreover, the solidarity and resilience displayed during such times reinforce national unity and pride, reminding citizens of their collective strength and compassion.

In addition to providing direct benefits, volunteerism also has a significant educational component. Many organizations that facilitate volunteer activities offer training and workshops that enhance the volunteers' skills, which they can then apply in various aspects of their lives. This training not only improves the effectiveness of their volunteer efforts but also contributes to their personal and professional development.

Community service initiatives are particularly effective in promoting civic engagement among youth. Schools and universities often encourage or require students to engage in community service as part of their education. This early exposure to volunteerism can instill a lifelong commitment to giving back to the community. Furthermore, it helps young people develop leadership skills, boosts their self-esteem, and enhances their resumes, which can be beneficial for their future career prospects.

The government can play a pivotal role in promoting volunteerism by providing support and recognition for volunteers and their organizations. This can include financial grants, resources for training, and national recognition programs that honor outstanding service contributions. By endorsing volunteerism, governments not only enhance the effectiveness of these activities but also signal the value of civic engagement to the entire nation.

Corporations and businesses also contribute to promoting

volunteerism through corporate social responsibility (CSR) programs. These programs often encourage employees to participate in community service activities, sometimes offering paid leave for this purpose. By integrating service into their business models, companies can contribute positively to societal welfare while fostering team spirit and employee satisfaction.

The media, too, plays a crucial role in promoting volunteerism by highlighting the positive impact of volunteer activities and celebrating the stories of volunteers who make a difference. Such coverage can inspire more people to volunteer, expanding the reach and impact of volunteer efforts.

Volunteerism and service are foundational to the development and strength of any nation. They enrich the lives of both givers and receivers by fostering a spirit of cooperation and mutual aid. Through these acts of service, citizens not only address pressing social needs but also build a stronger, more cohesive society. By nurturing a culture of volunteerism, a nation invests in its own future, ensuring that its citizens are ready and willing to support one another in times of need and everyday life alike.

• • •

"In every community service act, no matter how small, there lies the seed of national transformation. Each act of kindness is a thread in the fabric of our society. Let's weave a tapestry of service that covers and comforts all."

● ● ●

CHAPTER XVII

Overcoming Divisions: Addressing Regional and Ethnic Differences

In a world characterized by diversity, regional and ethnic differences can both enrich a society and present significant challenges to national unity. Addressing these differences effectively is crucial for fostering a cohesive society that values the contributions of all its members, regardless of their background. This endeavor requires a multi-faceted approach, encompassing policy, education, dialogue, and a commitment to equality and justice.

One of the primary methods of addressing regional and ethnic differences is through inclusive governance. Ensuring that all groups have representation in government decision-making processes is fundamental to fostering trust and cooperation. This can involve the implementation of proportional representation, decentralization of power, and the establishment of regional councils that allow for local governance. Such measures ensure that diverse communities can have a say in the laws and policies that affect their lives, reducing feelings of disenfranchisement and marginalization.

Education plays a pivotal role in overcoming divisions. Curricula that embrace multicultural education and teach about the history, cultures, and contributions of various ethnic and regional groups can cultivate understanding and respect among young citizens. Schools can serve as important venues for cross-cultural interaction and learning, where students from different backgrounds can come together and form bonds that last a lifetime. Educational programs should also include conflict resolution skills, which prepare students to navigate and mitigate disputes in a constructive manner.

Fostering economic equity is another crucial element in addressing regional and ethnic divisions. Economic disparities often underlie social tensions, with marginalized groups suffering from higher rates of poverty and limited access to opportunities. Government initiatives aimed at economic development in underprivileged areas can help rectify these imbalances. Such initiatives can include investment in education, infrastructure, health care, and job creation, ensuring that all regions and communities have the tools to thrive economically.

Cultural exchange programs within a country can also help bridge differences by promoting understanding and appreciation of diverse cultures. Festivals, art exhibits, and exchange visits between members of different regions or ethnic groups can enhance mutual respect and shared national identity. These interactions highlight commonalities and celebrate the unique aspects of each culture, fostering a more inclusive national narrative.

Dialogue and reconciliation processes are vital when there have been historical grievances or conflicts. These processes can involve truth and reconciliation commissions, public apologies, and reparations. They provide a platform for acknowledgment of past injustices and pave the way for healing and building a common future. Effective dialogue requires honest communication and a willingness from all sides to listen and understand each other's perspectives and experiences.

Media also plays a significant role in addressing regional and ethnic differences. Responsible media that strives to present balanced news coverage and features stories that promote unity rather than division can have a powerful impact on public perception and attitudes. Media initiatives that highlight success stories of integration and cooperation can inspire similar efforts elsewhere and help normalize the celebration of diversity.

Legal frameworks that protect the rights of all citizens, regardless of their ethnic or regional background, are fundamental to overcoming divisions. Laws that enforce equal treatment and protect against discrimination are essential for building a fair society. The judiciary plays a crucial role in upholding these laws, ensuring that justice is served when violations occur, and maintaining the rule of law.

Community leadership is equally important. Leaders who promote peace and unity, who are willing to engage in dialogue and cooperation with other groups, can have a profound impact at the local level. These leaders can act as role models and advocates for community-based solutions to ethnic and regional conflicts.

Addressing regional and ethnic differences requires a sustained and comprehensive approach that involves governance, education, economic development, cultural exchange, dialogue, media responsibility, legal protection, and community leadership. By embracing these strategies, a nation can move towards greater social cohesion, ensuring that all its citizens feel valued and integrated into the fabric of society. This commitment to unity in diversity is not only a moral imperative but also a practical one, as it strengthens the social fabric and enhances the nation's resilience and prosperity.

* * *

"Economic disparities within a nation are not just challenges to be overcome but opportunities to demonstrate our commitment to fairness and equality. By addressing these disparities, we strengthen the very foundation of our nation. Let's build an economy that uplifts every citizen."

• • •

CHAPTER XVIII

Economic Empowerment: Growing Together as a Nation

Economic empowerment is fundamental to building a strong, resilient, and unified nation. It involves creating an environment where all citizens have the opportunity to contribute to and benefit from economic growth. This goal can be achieved through policies and practices that ensure equitable access to resources, education, and employment, thereby fostering an inclusive economy that benefits every segment of society.

The foundation of economic empowerment is education and skill development. By investing in quality education for all citizens, a nation can develop a skilled workforce ready to meet the demands of the modern economy. This includes not only traditional schooling but also vocational training and adult education programs that equip individuals with practical skills that are in demand in the labor market. Such initiatives help reduce unemployment and underemployment, especially among young people and marginalized communities, and are crucial for economic growth and stability.

Financial inclusion is another critical aspect of economic empowerment. Access to financial services, such as banking, credit, insurance, and pensions, is essential for individuals and businesses to manage their finances, invest in opportunities, and protect themselves against economic shocks. Governments and financial institutions can promote financial inclusion by expanding services to underserved areas, offering microfinance options, and supporting financial literacy programs. These measures help individuals and small businesses to capitalize on economic opportunities, contributing to broader economic development.

Supporting entrepreneurship and small businesses is vital for economic empowerment. Small and medium enterprises (SMEs) are often major contributors to job creation and economic growth. By providing access to capital, business training, and market opportunities, governments and organizations can empower entrepreneurs to start and grow their businesses. Additionally, policies that reduce bureaucratic red tape and create a favorable business environment can encourage innovation and investment, driving economic growth and diversification.

Gender equality in economic participation also plays a significant role in economic empowerment. Ensuring that women have equal opportunities to participate in the economy can dramatically boost a nation's economic performance. This can be facilitated through policies that support women entrepreneurs, laws that ensure equal pay for equal work, and programs that encourage girls and women to pursue education and careers in high-paying sectors. Empowering women economically not only improves their personal and family well-being but also contributes to the overall health and productivity of the economy.

Labor rights and fair working conditions are crucial for sustainable economic growth. Protecting the rights of workers, ensuring fair wages, and providing safe working conditions are fundamental to maintaining a productive and satisfied workforce. Strong labor laws and effective enforcement mechanisms can prevent exploitation and ensure that the benefits of economic growth are shared equitably among workers and employers alike.

Economic diversification is important for a nation's resilience. Relying on a single industry or commodity can leave an economy vulnerable to market fluctuations and external shocks. By promoting diversification across various sectors—such as agriculture, manufacturing, services, and technology—countries can stabilize their economies and create a range of employment opportunities for their citizens. This not only helps in weathering economic downturns but also supports sustainable long-term growth.

Investment in infrastructure is another key driver of economic empowerment. Well-planned infrastructure, including transportation, telecommunications, energy, and public utilities, enhances productivity and connects markets. It also creates jobs and improves the quality of life by providing citizens with access to essential services. Government investment in infrastructure, particularly in underserved regions, can stimulate economic activities and help integrate different parts of the country into the national economy.

Economic empowerment involves a comprehensive approach that integrates education, financial inclusion, support for entrepreneurship, gender equality, labor rights, economic diversification, and infrastructure development. By implementing policies and initiatives that address these areas, a nation can ensure that its economic growth is inclusive and sustainable. This not only improves the living standards of its citizens but also fosters a sense of shared success and unity, essential for the long-term prosperity and cohesion of the society.

• • •

"The challenge of our times is to maintain optimism in the face of adversity. Positive thinking is not about ignoring the complexities of reality—it's about facing them with courage and hope. Let this positive outlook be our guide through stormy seas."

• • •

CHAPTER XIX

Global Perspectives: How the World Sees Us

Understanding how a nation is perceived internationally is crucial for its global standing and relations. These perceptions can influence foreign investment, tourism, diplomatic relations, and even the socio-economic opportunities available to its citizens abroad. Given the interconnected nature of today's world, managing and improving global perceptions has become a strategic priority for many countries.

The roots of international perception often lie in a nation's history, culture, political landscape, and economic performance. These elements combine to form a narrative that the rest of the world uses to interpret the identity and behavior of a nation. For instance, historical acts such as participation in global conflicts or colonialism can have long-lasting effects on a nation's image. Similarly, cultural exports like music, film, and cuisine can enhance a country's global reputation, creating a perception of vibrancy and appeal.

The role of media, both traditional and social, cannot be overstated in shaping global perspectives. International news outlets often focus on significant political or social events, and these stories can dominate the global narrative about a nation. Positive coverage, such as successful handling of a crisis or technological breakthroughs, can enhance a country's reputation, while negative coverage can lead to stereotypes and misconceptions. Social media amplifies this effect by providing a platform for instantaneous, widespread dissemination of information and opinions, which can quickly change a nation's image for better or worse.

Diplomacy is another critical factor in shaping how the world sees a country. Through international relations, countries can establish themselves as leaders, partners, or adversaries. Diplomatic efforts, such as peace negotiations, international aid, or active participation in global organizations, can significantly improve a nation's global standing. Conversely, isolationist policies or conflicts with other countries can tarnish a nation's image. The professionalism and demeanor of diplomatic representatives also play a key role in influencing perceptions.

Economic policies and performance also significantly affect international perceptions. A strong, stable economy can make a country appear reliable and prosperous, attractive for tourists, investors, and international business. Economic instability, on the other hand, can lead to perceptions of risk that deter investment and engagement. Policies that promote innovation, sustainability, and fair trade are particularly well-regarded on the global stage, as they reflect a commitment to progressive and responsible global citizenship.

Tourism is a powerful avenue for shaping global perceptions. By welcoming tourists, a country can showcase its best qualities, including natural landscapes, cultural sites, and hospitality. Positive experiences can lead to word-of-mouth endorsements and repeat visits, which bolster a nation's image. The strategy for tourism development, including marketing campaigns and infrastructure development, plays a significant role in how successful a country is at shaping these perceptions.

Cultural diplomacy, including international cultural festivals, exhibitions, and exchanges, allows countries to share their heritage and modern artistic expressions with an international audience. These interactions not only foster a deeper understanding and appreciation of a nation's culture but also build bridges between peoples, which can counteract stereotypes and promote a more nuanced view of the nation.

Educational exchanges and scholarships offered to international students also serve as significant diplomatic tools. They enable people from different countries to experience the culture, values, and educational strengths of a host nation firsthand. Alumni of these programs often become informal ambassadors for the country, sharing their positive experiences and insights with others in their home countries.

Global perceptions are shaped by a complex mix of historical legacy, media representation, diplomatic engagement, economic performance, tourism, cultural diplomacy, and educational exchanges. Managing these perceptions requires a coordinated effort across multiple domains to ensure that the image projected abroad aligns with the nation's values and aspirations. By actively engaging in the global dialogue and presenting a positive, authentic, and multifaceted image, a country can enhance how it is perceived worldwide, leading to increased respect, cooperation, and opportunities on the international stage.

• • •

"Global perspectives enrich our national identity; they teach us how others see us and how we see ourselves in the global community. Let's embrace these perspectives to enhance our understanding and our contributions to the world. Every international interaction is a chapter in our nation's story."

• • •

CHAPTER XX

Looking Forward: The Future of National Unity and Positive Thinking

As nations navigate the complexities of modern geopolitics, economic fluctuations, and societal changes, the ideals of national unity and positive thinking are more vital than ever. These principles serve not only as a beacon of hope but also as practical strategies for fostering social cohesion and sustainable development. Looking forward, the challenge for nations is to cultivate these ideals systematically and inclusively, ensuring that every citizen can contribute to and benefit from a unified national agenda.

Integrating Technology and Innovation

The future of national unity can be significantly enhanced by embracing technological advancements and innovation. Digital platforms can bridge geographical and social gaps by providing forums for dialogue and exchange across diverse populations. Initiatives like e-governance can streamline interactions between citizens and the government, enhancing transparency and trust. Furthermore, technology can be used to promote cultural heritage and national achievements, creating a shared sense of pride and identity.

Investments in technology should also focus on educational technologies that foster a comprehensive understanding of national history, civic responsibilities, and cultural diversity. Virtual reality experiences, interactive simulations, and online learning platforms can make learning about these topics more engaging and accessible to a broad audience.

Promoting Inclusive Growth

Economic strategies that prioritize inclusivity and equitable growth are fundamental to the future of national unity. Policies should aim to reduce disparities by investing in underdeveloped regions and supporting marginalized communities. Economic empowerment through education, job creation, and entrepreneurship opportunities can help integrate diverse groups into the national economy, reducing social tensions and building a sense of shared purpose.

In addition, fostering a business environment that encourages innovation and sustainability can attract investment and promote a more dynamic economy. Such an environment not only strengthens the economic foundations of a nation but also showcases its commitment to responsible and inclusive growth on the global stage.

Enhancing Social Policies

The future of national unity relies heavily on robust social policies that address the needs of all citizens. Healthcare, housing, and social welfare programs that are accessible and fair can alleviate the stresses that often divide communities. These policies should be designed with the input of the communities they aim to serve, ensuring that they are responsive and effective.

Mental health is an area that deserves particular attention. Promoting mental wellness and positive thinking through national health initiatives can improve overall societal health and productivity. Programs that emphasize resilience, stress management, and emotional intelligence can equip citizens to handle personal and communal challenges more effectively.

Cultivating Civic Engagement

Encouraging active civic engagement is essential for sustaining national unity. This can be achieved by making civic education a cornerstone of the educational system and by creating opportunities for citizens to engage in community service and decision-making processes. Platforms that allow citizens to contribute their ideas and feedback on national projects can make governance more participatory and democratic.

Promoting Cultural and Ethical Values

A nation's culture and ethics play a crucial role in unifying its people. Promoting values such as respect, integrity, and cooperation through media, arts, and education can help inculcate a national ethos that aligns with the ideals of unity and positivity. Celebrating cultural diversity through festivals, arts, and educational programs can enhance understanding and appreciation among different ethnic and regional groups.

Looking to the Future with Optimism

The future of national unity and positive thinking must involve a proactive and optimistic approach to global challenges. Preparing for future challenges through adaptive and forward-thinking policies will be crucial. This includes not only addressing immediate concerns such as economic stability and social welfare but also anticipating future issues such as climate change and technological disruptions.

The future of national unity and positive thinking is an ongoing journey that requires continuous effort and adaptation. By leveraging technology, promoting inclusive growth, enhancing social policies, cultivating civic engagement, and upholding cultural and ethical values, nations can build a resilient and unified future.

This vision for the future is not only about preserving harmony and prosperity but also about inspiring and empowering every citizen to contribute positively to their nation and the world.

• • •

"Looking forward, let's not just anticipate changes but actively participate in shaping them. The future of our nation depends not on the few but on the many. Let's all contribute to a narrative of unity and positivity, paving the way for a prosperous tomorrow."

• • •

CHAPTER XXI

SUMMARY

As we journey through the exploration of "Patriotic Spirits: Inspiring a Nation Through Positive Thinking," we delve into the multifaceted relationships between patriotism, national identity, and the power of positive thinking. This book offers a comprehensive examination of how these elements can intertwine to foster national unity and propel countries towards social harmony and progressive development. Each chapter provides insights into different aspects of how positive thinking and patriotism can be harnessed to enhance both individual lives and the collective societal experience.

The Roots of Patriotism explores the fundamental origins of national identity and how historical narratives, cultural heritage, and shared values shape our understanding of patriotism. It discusses the importance of history in forming a patriotic consciousness and how this awareness fosters a connection among citizens that transcends generations.

Pride in the Past addresses the significance of historical events and figures in shaping national pride. By celebrating historical milestones and learning from past struggles, nations can cultivate a sense of shared identity and pride that is crucial for long-term unity and resilience.

Unity in Diversity examines how embracing cultural, ethnic, and regional differences within a nation can strengthen societal bonds. This chapter underscores the importance of inclusivity and respect for diversity as key components of a healthy and unified national identity.

The Power of Positivity focuses on the impact of a positive mindset in shaping national attitudes and public policies. It highlights how optimism and constructive thinking can lead to effective problem-solving and enhanced societal well-being.

Women at the Forefront recognizes the pivotal role of female leadership in national development. This chapter celebrates the contributions of women across various sectors and discusses the need for gender equality in fostering comprehensive national progress.

Youth and Patriotism discusses the critical role of the younger generation in sustaining national ideals and introduces ways to engage youth in patriotism through education, media, and civic activities.

Symbols of Pride delves into how national symbols and rituals can foster a sense of community and pride among citizens, serving as unifying elements that reinforce national values and history.

Voices of Change highlights inspirational stories of national figures who have influenced their countries through acts of bravery, innovation, and leadership. These narratives serve as powerful motivators for current and future generations.

Education for Empowerment argues for the pivotal role of education in fostering patriotism and preparing citizens to contribute positively to their nation. It stresses the need for educational systems that promote civic responsibility and national pride.

Community Spirit emphasizes the importance of local community engagement in building national unity. It explores how grassroots initiatives and local governance can enhance social cohesion.

The Role of Media examines the media's power in shaping public perception and national sentiment. It discusses the responsibility of the media to promote positive narratives that contribute to a unified national identity.

Arts and Patriotism explores how artistic expressions can reflect and enhance national pride and identity, serving as both a mirror and a mold for patriotic sentiments.

Technology for Unity looks at how digital tools and platforms can bring people together, enhance communication, and foster a sense of national community in an increasingly digital world.

Environmental Patriotism discusses the integration of environmental conservation into the patriotic ethos, emphasizing the importance of protecting natural heritage as a form of national pride and responsibility.

Celebrations of Unity reflects on the role of national holidays in strengthening communal bonds and reinforcing national values through shared celebrations and remembrances.

Volunteerism and Service highlights the importance of civic engagement and volunteer work in promoting national unity and social welfare, showcasing how giving back to the community strengthens societal bonds.

Overcoming Divisions addresses the challenges of regional and ethnic differences within nations, proposing pathways to reconciliation and unity through inclusive policies and practices.

Economic Empowerment explores how economic policies focused on inclusivity and equitable growth can strengthen national unity by ensuring that all citizens have the opportunity to contribute to and benefit from the national economy.

Global Perspectives discusses the international implications of national identity and how a country's global image can influence its diplomatic and economic interactions.

Looking Forward concludes with a visionary outlook on the future of national unity and positive thinking, emphasizing proactive and inclusive strategies to navigate the challenges of modern societies.

In summary, this book provides a deep dive into the powerful interplay between patriotism and positive thinking, offering a blueprint for building stronger, more unified nations. It invites readers to consider how individual attitudes and actions can contribute to the broader narrative of national unity and progress, emphasizing the importance of collective responsibility in shaping a prosperous and harmonious future.

• • •

Citation And References

This book represents the culmination of extensive research and meticulous analysis, incorporating a diverse range of sources, including numerous books, scholarly studies, and personal experiences. Additionally, I have scoured various websites to gather relevant information and data essential for the compilation of this work. I have taken every precaution to ensure the accuracy of the information presented and have diligently cited all sources to acknowledge their contributions.

Despite these efforts, the possibility of inadvertent errors remains. I deeply value the insights of my readers and appreciate any feedback that can help identify and rectify such inaccuracies. I encourage you to bring any discrepancies to my attention.

Your feedback is not only welcome but crucial, as it will aid in correcting current editions and enhancing the content of future ones. I am committed to maintaining the highest standards of accuracy and reliability in my work and thank you for your support and understanding.

Additionally, I firmly uphold the principle of freedom of speech and expression as guaranteed under Article 19(1)(a) of the Constitution of India, and I respect the diverse viewpoints and expressions of all readers.

• • •

Other Books Of The Author

1. Empowering Minds: A Journey into Women's Self-Discovery and Power
2. The Dynamics of Motivation: Catalyzing Thought into Action
3. Meditation and Mental Well Being: The Path to Inner Peace and Clarity
4. The Psychology of Child Education: Nurturing Future Generations
5. Ethical Enlightenment: A Modern Guide to Living with Integrity
6. Voices of Empowerment: Stories of Women Rising Against Odds
7. Social Psychology in Everyday Life: Understanding Human Connections
8. The Essence of Motivational Speaking: Inspiring Change in Others
9. Balancing Acts: Women, Work, and the Will to Lead
10. Guiding with Grace: Raising Children with Compassion and Awareness
11. The Power of Positive Aging: Embracing Life After Fifty
12. Building Resilient Communities: Social Work in Action
13. The Ethical Educator: Principles for Teaching and Learning
14. From Insight to Impact: Social Psychology for a Better World
15. The Ethics of Empathy: A Guide to Ethical Living
16. The Science of Empowering the Self: Navigating Life's Challenges with Psychological Wisdom
17. The Mindful Conscious Leader: Meditation Techniques for Modern Management
18. Pioneering Spirit: Women's Pathways to Leadership and Empowerment
19. Feeling to Healing: The Role of Emotional Intelligence in Child Development
20. Transformative Talks and Words of Inspiration: Insights into Motivational Oratory

• • •

Contact

Dr. Minakshi Bansal
Social Activist
Ahmedabad, Gujarat, Bharat
minakshiindiag20@yahoo.com

• • •

|| LOKAHA SAMASTHAHA SUKHINO BHAVANTU ||

131